Baby Otter

AT HOME IN THE BAY

WRITTEN BY JENNIFER BOUDART
ILLUSTRATED BY MARK FRUEH

Publications International, Ltd.

Up, down, and up again. Waves rock Mother Sea Otter and her little pup. Mother Otter floats on her back. Baby Otter curls himself up tightly against his mother's chest. He is just a few hours old.

His mother's soft body, the safety of her arms, the rocking of the sea . . . this is all that the little pup knows.

It's time for Baby Otter to learn about the world around him. His mother pushes him into the water. The two float together, bellies up. The pup's thick fur keeps him warm.

Baby Otter kicks his webbed feet and splashes Mother Otter. What fun! The youngster learns some great new tricks during his first swim.

Baby Otter is learning quickly. He can swim easily on his back. It is good practice for Baby Otter because sea otters spend most of their lives in water.

Baby Otter's mother must dive for food. Before she goes, she wraps up Baby Otter in the kelp. The plants hold him so he does not float away. Down goes his mother, into the kelp forest.

This is Baby Otter's first time without Mother Otter at his side. He lies very still. A gull lands on a rock near him. Baby Otter is interested in the strange bird. The gull ignores him. She cleans her feathers with her beak.

Then Mother Otter comes back. She chatters at the gull, knowing the bird will try to steal her food. The gull flies away.

Mother Otter brings food up from the bottom of the ocean. Sometimes she will bring up a rock, tucking it under her arm. When her teeth cannot open a shell, she rests the rock on her chest and uses it to crack open the shell. Pound! Pound!

Baby Otter is still too young for this food. His mother's milk is all he needs. 🐾🐾

Mother Otter grooms her baby after every meal. She uses her paws, teeth, and tongue. Clean fur is very important. If an otter has dirty fur, then the cold water can soak in.

Baby Otter is now very sleepy. He takes a nap, and his mother watches for danger. She uses a paw to shade her eyes from the bright sun.

Baby Otter wakes up to a new and exciting world! He watches a brown pelican scooping up fish. He does not see the eagle flying above him. Mother Otter does, so she dives with him to safety.

Baby Otter holds his breath. He is very frightened. This is his first dive. In a moment, he is carried to the water's surface. The eagle has flown away.

The danger is finally gone. Baby Otter and his mother join other mothers and their pups. Baby Otter makes many friends. Together they wrestle, play with bits of seaweed, and dunk each other in the water.

Then a harbor seal swims by Baby Otter. The seal's whiskers brush his in a friendly kiss, and she is gone. 🐾 🐾

Suddenly, strong winds and rain arrive. Mother Otter and her baby swim away from the other otters to find shelter.

The wild waves rise higher. Baby Otter squeaks loudly as he and Mother Otter ride the waves. His mother calms him with soft humming noises and holds onto him tightly until the storm ends. 🐾 🐾

What a very special day for Baby Otter! He went for his first swim, met his first danger, and made his first friends in the bay. Baby Otter drifts off to sleep as he watches the moon rise. 🐾🐾